GLASTONBURY FESTIVAL
MYTHS & LEGENDS

BY MARC LEVERTON

◆ Tangent Books

Glastonbury Festival Myths and Legends by Marc Leverton

First published in 2013 by Tangent Books
Unit 5.16 Paintworks
Bristol BS4 3EH
0117 977 0645
www.tangentbooks.co.uk

978-1-906477-86-8

Publisher: Richard Jones richard@tangentbooks.co.uk
Design: Joe Burt joe@wildsparkdesign.co.uk

A CIP record for this book is available from the British Library.

Printed by Short Run Press, Exeter using paper from sustainable sources.

INTRODUCTION

Britain has a history far weirder than most history books recognise, strange people with bizarre beliefs and unusual customs have been roaming these lands for centuries. Nowadays the descendants of these nutters pay homage to their ancestors by camping in a field for a few days, listening to loud rock 'n' roll, drinking cider and yelling 'Bollocks' as loud as they can.

The Glastonbury Festival of Contemporary Performing Arts is held in a region with more myths and legends per square inch than any other part of the UK. They say you can't throw a wellie without hitting a ley line in Somerset. The Festival itself has generated many myths and legends. Stories of debauchery, squalor and filth contrast with tales of compassion, connection and an inebriated appreciation of our fellow raver.

This book collects the weird, the wonderful and the funniest of these myths and legends to form a celebration of the few days of merriment and madness that make the Festival unique.

Marc Leverton, Avalon, 2013

CONTENTS

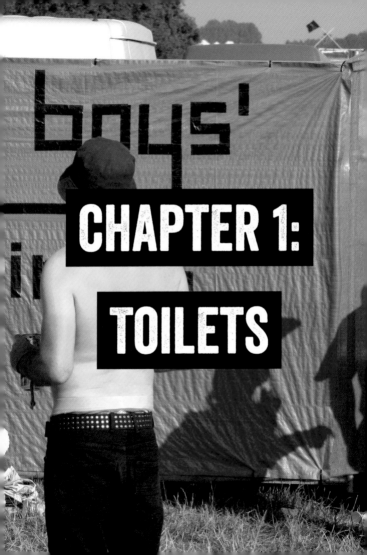

CHAPTER 1:

TOILETS

SHIT HITS THE FANS

During a very hot year the burly farmer boys who usually suck all the crap out the bogs were instead spraying water on the tracks to stop dust kicking up. Some clot accidentally pulled the wrong lever and sprayed a group of sun-worshipping Festival-goers in warm shit and piss.

CRAP STRIKES TWICE

One muddy year the dance tent was swimming in a pool of mud so deep that someone sent in the tractor boys, whether it was the same clot remains unknown but the wrong lever was pulled again. The dance tent was closed for several hours.

I AM IN THE LOO...

Some desperate punters without tickets were on their way to the Festival when they spotted their opportunity. At a service station they saw a lorry loaded with portable toilets. After a long and bumpy ride through the night on a toilet seat, finally they heard the truck stop. Deciding they must have arrived, they jumped free of their plastic cells, only to find themselves smack bang in the middle of the security area.

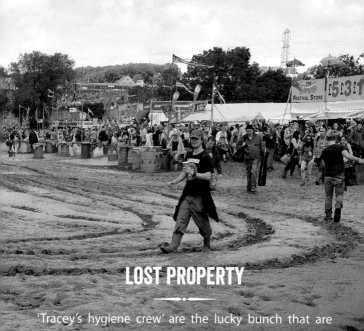

LOST PROPERTY

——— ◆ ———

'Tracey's hygiene crew' are the lucky bunch that are
tasked with clearing up the bogs. All the 'waste' is taken
up to 'the lagoon' where it is sifted before going to the
sewage works. They've found false teeth, presumably
thrown up by merry Festival-goers who have consumed
one too many shandys and of course many mobile
phones are dropped into the sea of smelly effluent.
However, their greatest find to date is a false leg, which
they have optimistically held on to, but is yet to be

WE HAVE ALL GOT TO GO SOMETIME...

The only recorded death in a Glastonbury toilet is that of Christopher Shale, a close friend of David Cameron and chairman of the West Oxfordshire Conservative Association. The 56-year-old died in a portaloo behind the Pyramid Stage in 2011. He is believed to have suffered a heart attack.

GOLD MEDAL TOILETS

The Glastonbury toilets often come in for a lot of stick, but the sheer feat of providing so many facilities for so many with so little environmental impact has been recognised and festival organisers have advised charities working in crisis areas in Africa on sanitation.

The story that there was no festival in 2012 because all the UK's portaloos were headed to London for the Olympics was dispelled by Michael Eavis as a myth.

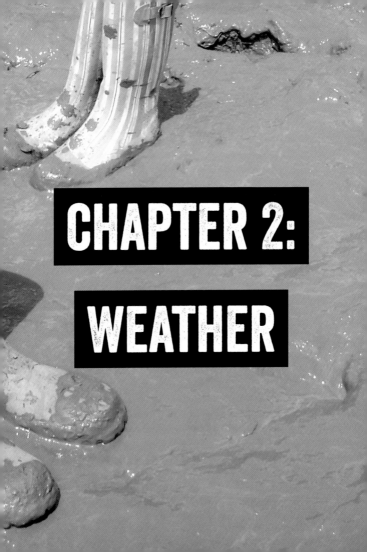

CHAPTER 2:

WEATHER

CLOUDBUSTING

Artists are forever making outlandish requests, but Sir Paul McCartney went one further when he asked Michael Eavis to do something about the weather which threatened his set. Undeterred, the ever-obliging Mr Eavis brought a home-made 'cloudbusting' machine out of retirement which had been gathering dust since the early 70s. Eavis was reported as saying "I had a call from Sir Paul's people saying, 'what are you doing about the rain?' This thing looks like an aircraft gun and you point it at the clouds. It is all done through the orgone energy thing Reich believed in."

Cloudbusting

Kate Bush

Wilhelm Reich was an Austrian physician who claimed to have discovered the 'unknown energy which exists in all living matter' – namely Orgone, the target of the cloudbusting machine. Kate Bush released a single called *Cloudbusting* in 1985.

RAIN, RAIN, GO AWAY

There have been several 'muddy years' but in 2005 the torrential rain was so severe that several lagoons, lakes and rivers wreaked chaos across the site making more than 100 people 'homeless'. The British sense of humour will never be dampened however and one wag rechristened what was left of his abode 'Riverside Cottage'. Many Festival-goers splashed around in the lagoons, until they noticed the upturned portaloos upstream.

SINGING 'LAGER, LAGER, LAGER'

A puzzled crowd gathered to watch a man diving into a deep brown pool of muddy water. Assuming that he would resurface with camping essentials such as his sleeping bag, tent or boots, a huge cheer erupted as he triumphantly emerged with his weekend supply of lager.

During that same year the Street Sub Aqua Club (pictured) were called in to check that the submerged tents didn't have anyone in them, thankfully they didn't.

CLUB FOOT

Keeping your boots on when the ground is a quagmire would appear the logical thing to do. However, several cases of trench foot have been recorded at the Festival over the years. The condition is most commonly associated with World War One when soldiers' feet were subjected to prolonged wetness and would go mouldy. If left untreated trench foot can result in the loss of nails, toes or even result in complete amputation.

RED SKY AT NIGHT

Farmers have many myths and legends surrounding weather predictions, most notably the 'Red sky at night, shepherd's delight' saying. But did you know that cows do not like the wind in their faces, and so they will typically stand with their backs to the wind? Since a western wind typically means good weather and eastern winds usually indicate unsettled weather, the direction that your cows are standing is a fairly accurate forecast. Unlike the belief that if cows are sitting down then rain is on its way, that was disproved by *Tomorrow's World*. Apparently Michael Eavis doesn't rely on any ancient wisdom, and is said to avoid all weather predictions until the festival starts.

SNOW SAVES LOCAL OXFAM

The nearby Oxfam shop in Bridgwater was earmarked for closure due to increasing High Street rents. A concerned volunteer wrote to Michael Eavis to see if there was anything he could do to help. Luckily the farm was under snow, and because Mr Eavis was at a loose end, he took up the cause. Using his contacts at Oxfam (and reminding them of the £300,000 donation that the festival makes to the charity each year) he was able to save the shop. He also took it upon himself to negotiate with the landlord over the proposed rent increase and find a sponsor to pay the rent for the next few years. At the re-opening of the shop, one over keen volunteer is said to have taken Eavis' coat thinking it was a donation and put it on for sale for £9.99.

CHAPTER 3:

ORGANISED

CHAOS

FENCE JUMPERS

In 2000, the niggling small stream of fence-jumpers became a raging torrent as an estimated 150,000 extra people joined the already sold-out party. This led to an edgy Festival with more than average levels of scousers, gang members, petty thieves, drug dealers and blaggers joining the party.

On another occasion security officers were tipped off about a scam in which gatecrashers plotted to impersonate paramedics by arriving in an ambulance. This resulted in searches of every emergency vehicle entering the site.

WALL

OVER IT

THE RING OF STEEL

The 'ring of steel' is the pet name given to the toughest temporary fence in the world. Eavis got busy after persistent fence jumpers threatened the future of the Festival. Legend has it that the fence can be seen from space. Unfortunately, Bono didn't take the opportunity to confirm this when he spoke with an astronaut from the Pyramid stage during U2's set.

THE BATTLE OF YEOMAN'S BRIDGE

Many point to the travellers' riot in the late 80s as the point when 'the modern music festival' was born. Michael Eavis had tolerated their presence for many years, despite their refusal to pay and their tendency to hang around after the Festival. A scuffle, a burnt out temporary building and a face-off with security and police was enough aggro for Eavis to declare a 'fallow year'. When the Festival returned there was no longer a travellers' field. The old travellers' field is now part of Shangri-La, a whole new world of crazy.

THE MAN WHO FELL TO EARTH

Only one person managed to scale the new 15-foot high super-fence in its first year. Unfortunately, this person's mates weren't made of such stern stuff and couldn't make it over. So, despite his Herculean efforts, he jumped back over to be with his chums.

One person who did make it in that year was a parachutist who descended into the middle of the crowd. Festival staff described Monty Python-esque scenes as groups of furious security men tried to reach the mystery person, only to find themselves blocked by the crowd. Members of the crowd took his chute and hid it in a tent to allow the action man to blend in.

TENTS FOR AFRICA

Every year Festival-goers leave behind increasing amounts of cheap camping paraphernalia. Many believe that these tents are collected and distributed to charitable groups working in Africa. Unfortunately, the cost of collecting the tents, cleaning and repairing them and sending them overseas is too great and most of them simply end up in landfill. Hence the Festival slogan 'Love the Farm, Leave no Trace'.

EAU DE EAVIS

To many the ultimate symbol of success is a swimming pool. Palm trees, sun loungers and Playgirls could adorn a private, heated pool. Not in Mr Eavis' case though. His unheated pool is in a cowshed, where he swims 24 lengths each morning.

It would be out of character for the swimming pool to just have one use, and supposedly the pool also doubles as the storage for the drinking water for the Festival. Presumably it is filtered before we drink it.

WILD WEST

The market area is now a peaceful area for traders to coin it by selling wellies and crystal Buddhas, but back in the 1980s market traders were regularly 'taxed' by semi-organised gangs wielding pick axes. One of the solutions to this problem came in the form of changing the layout of the markets from a 'street' to a 'wagon train' formation. Essentially forming the markets in a circular shape akin to the wagon trains of the wild west under attack from 'injuns'.

I'M A BACK DOOR MAN

Entering and leaving the Festival is often a nightmare (or part of the experience depending on your view). Stories abound of being stuck out on country lanes for nine hours, or being dropped off by a bus 'outside' the Festival only to find it takes another three hours of dragging your gear through muddy puddles and ditches before you finally reach the gate.

Of course there is always some cocky sod 'in the know' who says 'Oh, you should have come around the back of Shepton Mallet. It only took me half an hour from my front door, and I live in Newcastle'. The same cocky sod will probably tell you they saw Radiohead play in a secret backstage area, or of a mythical camping area where there is no mud.

THE BEST VIEW IN THE HOUSE

Who gets the best view of the Pyramid stage during the Festival? The best seat in the house probably belongs to Julian Temperley founder of Burrow Hill Cider whose

Somerset Cider Bus overlooks the Pyramid Stage. His gaff for the Festival is on the top floor of the bus, in which he has a double bed where he claims he sleeps better than at home. Obviously that would have nothing to do with the cider fumes.

CHAPTER 4:
WEIRD AND
WONDERFUL

WALK THE LINE

Whilst creating the first ever Festival, the organisers knew the stage should be at the bottom of the hill, but where at the bottom of the hill? Cue Andrew Kerr, co-organiser and bona fide hippy drop-out who reached for his dowsing rod. The ancient art of dowsing revealed the course of the powerful St Michael ley line that runs through the site, extending from Glastonbury town right down to Stonehenge.

PYRAMID SONG

Kerr is also a strong believer in sacred geometry, which is the theory that buildings can be infused with energy. Glastonbury Tor and Abbey are both sites which have intrigued 'sacred archaeologists' over the years so it is fitting that the Festival should respect these traditions.

There is a mystical theory from a book called *The View Over Atlantis* that there is a sacred correlation between the dimensions of Stonehenge, the Pyramids of Egypt and Glastonbury Abbey. Its author Jean Michell is said to have joined Kerr before the first Festival and influenced his decision to use the Egyptian pyramid shape to harness the power of the ley lines. Given the many incredible performances from that stage over the years who could dispute their power?

CRYSTAL DAYS

A second version of the pyramid stage was built from scrap metal discarded by the Ministry of Defence, legend has it that is was the bad karma of its previous incarnation which led to it burning down. There is also a story that at the very apex of the pyramid someone put a crystal, which they bought from a hippy shop on Glastonbury High Street. Unfortunately, its powers couldn't prevent the mystery blaze.

Another myth is that Michael Eavis told the local council that the stage doubled as a cow shed in winter as a way of getting around planning laws, although a good story he has consistently denied this claim.

PARTY LIKE ITS 1999 (B.C.)

Glastonbury Festival is a chance for the modern reveller to cut loose and re-connect with their inner Keith Richards. What many don't realise is that there have been English folk festivals for many centuries. Religious festivals around the solstice go back even further than that, Christian cultures celebrate the feast of St John (June 24-25) and Pagans celebrate Midsummer Day on June 25th.

These types of community get-togethers celebrate the arrival of new seasons and often conjure ancient deities such as the god of Pan – the spirit of spring and fertility, and The Green Man – the symbol of rebirth. Another popular figure at the Festival is The Wicker Man whose roots can be traced to ancient Pagans and Celts who supposedly burnt similar effigies as part of an elaborate human sacrifice ritual.

THERE IS A LIGHT THAT NEVER GOES OUT

In the mid-90s, rumours spread like wildfire that Cliff Richard, now *Sir* Cliff Richard had left this mortal coil. Fortunately, especially for the Peter Pan of Pop, this was just a rumour and revellers emerged from the Festival to find him in good health.

The unfortunate death of a rock star or celebrity is a common rumour, and pre-mobile phone and internet these rumours were impossible to verify, which of course added to their potency. Other years saw Keith Richards and Michael Jackson take the honours. Which is why when Michael Jackson really did die, many laughed it off as just another 'Glastonbury rumour'.

FIRST FESTIVAL

1970 is well documented as the first Glastonbury Festival, Eavis having been inspired by seeing Led Zeppelin at the Bath Festival of Blues and Progressive Music at the Shepton Mallet Showground. Tickets for the first Festival were £1 which included a free pint of milk. The security that year was provided by a group of local Hell's Angels who upset organisers by making off with the ox roast.

What is not so well known is that there was another Glastonbury Fayre in the early part of the twentieth century. Curated by a gentleman called Rutland Boughton, the Fayre ran from 1914 to 1926 and was a

theatre and music event. The theme of the Fayre? Glastonbury's local 'myths and legends'. Boughton didn't reach the same level of success as Eavis. But it is interesting that both share a sometimes unpopular radicalism, and seem a little ahead of their time.

ARE WE THERE YET?

Seasoned Festival-goers eventually work out that Glastonbury Festival isn't actually in Glastonbury, it is closer to Shepton Mallet than to Glastonbury Town and the site is between Pilton and Pylle. So why is it called the Glastonbury Festival? Well, would you go to the Shepton Mallet Festival of Contemporary Performing Arts? Exactly. And why do locals call it Pilton Pop Festival? Well, that was the name of the first Festival.

WELCOME TO SOMERSET

Today's 'pilgrims' to the Festival join a long list of visitors to the area which includes St Patrick, ancient monks, Holy Grail hunters and Jesus Christ's uncle Joseph of Aramethea. Did a young Jesus accompany his uncle on one of his trips? Some people say so.

Glastonbury is a 'who's who' of mystery, legend and myth. King Arthur and Queen Guinevere are rumoured to be buried under the Tor. And what links Arthur to Jesus? Only the daddy of all myths – the Holy Grail. Don't even ask about UFO activity in the area.

THE DOGS DON'T WORK

Back in the day, the bridge to the stone circle was the place to get your, erm, recreational supplies. A steady chorus of 'aciiid' and 'black hash' would chime through the evening.

One nervous young punter approached a man who was yelling 'Mushroom, MUSHROOM' and asked to buy some of his merchandise. The man replied 'I'm not selling anything pal, I'm just calling me dog'.

FULL CIRCLE

The Stone Circle is not an ancient monument as some assume but was built in the early 90s by Ivan McBeth. Whilst searching for inspiration he camped out on the space and hit upon the idea of basing the layout of the stones on the Cygnet astral formation. Still doubting his idea he made a reluctant start, digging the holes for the stones by hand. A few days into his digging he heard a loud commotion hailing from the skies as seven swans flew overhead in formation. Needless to say, McBeth saw this as sign that his plan must be realised and pressed on with renewed faith in his idea.

RAGE AGAINST THE WASHING MACHINES

Many people suggest that the Festival isn't what it used to be, and the clientele are no longer the 'great unwashed' of days gone by. Perhaps the clearest illustration of this is the rumour that Mr Eavis is to install washing machines at the site to satisfy today's more demanding fans.

CHAPTER 5:

ARTISTES ONLY

BOGHENGE

The Stone Circle was built in the 90s to align with the summer solstice sunrise. A few years on and Banksy erected his 'Boghenge' lower down in the same field, using portaloos instead of sacred stones. Legend has it that Mr Eavis was unimpressed, as were the Health and Safety crew especially after the work became graffitied, pushed over and turned into the ruin that it was originally apeing.

THIS CHARMING KLAN

Journalists from the press tent hurried off to the main stage to see the Wu-Tang Clan's set on the strength of a rumour that they were about to perform with Morrissey. Unfortunately, this was indeed a rumour, and the world will never hear 'Irish blood, gangsta heart'.

RIDE BABY RIDE

Traditional rock 'n' roll riders might include drugs, alcohol, pornography and some groupies. But according to reliable tabloid reports (*Daily Mirror*), Coldplay's rider included two crates of filtered mineral water and an unlimited amount of crudités. They are also said to have requested an "assortment of vegetarian, gluten-free dips". Viva guacamole.

PEACE IN THE VALLEY

Roy Harper was a stalwart of the Festival in its early years, in many ways his peaceful acoustic troubadour persona embodies the early Festival spirit. He had a reputation for over-running and the next act on happened to be legendary Cream drummer Ginger Baker. Baker decided enough was enough and took to the stage to set up his drum kit. Like all good legends there are at least two versions of what happened next.

1. The fracas between Harper and Baker became fairly serious when Harper punched the drummer. Baker took it on the chin and carried on setting up anyway and Harper was carried off the stage kicking and screaming.

2. The audience of Harper fans were incensed by Baker's actions and his band were bottled during their first number. Baker was smashed in the head by a bottle, some reports say that Baker was then carried from the stage and taken to hospital. Others claim Baker didn't even miss a beat and carried on regardless of the bleeding head wound.

THE FIERCE AND THE FEARLESS

Much hoo-ha was made when Beyonce headlined the Festival, one of the claims being that she was the first woman to headline the event in 40 years. Some people pointed out that accolade actually belongs to 80s folky songstress Suzanne Vega, although it would seem impossible to compare the two artists.

However, legend has it that before her performance Vega was the unlikely target of a death threat. Why anyone would want to kill one of the least offensive people in rock remains a mystery.

Much to her credit she performed regardless of the threat. The legend is cemented by the fact that she performed her set wearing a bulletproof vest. Now that is fierce.

SOAP DODGERS

U2's headline performance sparked protests from a group called Art Uncut who wanted to highlight the issue that the band had taken its finances 'off shore' from Ireland to Holland in order to pay a lower rate of tax.

Rumours abounded that the intended protests included elaborate sieges of sound towers and a mass stage invasion. In reality, perhaps due to security or because of the heavy rain, or both, there was just this 24-metre balloon with its 'U pay tax 2?' slogan. The photo shows the balloon seconds before it was seized by security.

BLUE SUNDAY

Controversy over headline acts is nothing new to the Festival, in the early 80s New Order were favoured over hippy legends Hawkwind. A group of bikers rode through the audience and sat revving their bikes at the front of the stage throughout the terrified Mancunians entire set.

Although not headliners The Smiths were another controversial choice of act a few years later, but they won over a sceptical crowd with help from younger members of the audience who invaded the stage to dance.

In the 80s it seemed that Van Morrison played the Festival every year, so everyone assumed that the grumpy Irishman was a personal favourite of Michael Eavis. But in an 80s interview Eavis revealed that The Smiths set was his favourite Glastonbury performance to date. He later went on record as saying that The Smiths were the band 'who made Glastonbury fashionable'.

AT THE DRIVE-IN.

During the Brit pop years artist Damien Hirst found himself in a situation that all Festival-goers will sympathise with. Namely, being on one side of the Festival, and there being an epic journey between you and that band you would like to see. The difference for Damien however was that he had his Land Rover with him, so he simply drove through the Festival, through the crowd at the Jazz stage and parked up at the front of the stage in time for the performance.

SHAKE AND VAC

Despite the 'legendary' tales of drug abuse at the festival Michael Eavis has gone on record saying that he doesn't condone drug use in any way. Various tales crop up from time to time, such as the festivals recent refusal of an offer to test the effluent waste at the festival to calculate how much drug use is taking place. The weirdest story by far is that of the 'drugs vacuum' that was able to 'smell' illicit substances in a similar way to police dogs. The device was employed by Avon and Somerset Constabulary in the 90s and revellers recall a very real fear of being busted by a police officer holding something which must have looked like a Dyson.

GLASTONBURY BY NUMBERS

MONEY GENERATED FOR THE LOCAL ECONOMY EACH YEAR: £35 million

ARRESTS:
123 (2011)
109 (2010)

NUMBER OF BBC VIEWERS:
16 million

NUMBER OF BARS:
20

WATER ON SITE:
2 million litres

NUMBER OF COWS THAT LIVE AT THE FARM:
360 milking cows
200 calves

NUMBER OF PUNTERS:
2,000 (1970)
12,000 (1971)
18,000 (1981)
177,500 (2008)
137,616 (2011)

AMOUNT OF EFFLUENT PRODUCED:
700,000 gallons

SPEED TICKETS SOLD:
2 days (2003)
4 hours (2011)

THE FENCE: 15 feet high, 4 miles long

RELATIONSHIPS ENDED:
Don't even go there

FIRST AIDERS:
400

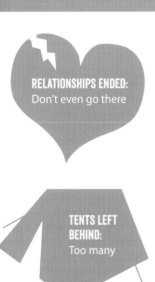

TENTS LEFT BEHIND:
Too many

PINTS OF MILK PRODUCED BY WORTHY FARM DAILY:
10,200 litres

NUMBER OF TOILETS:
4,500

Photo Credits
Many thanks to the talented photographers
whose images illustrate this book:

Daniel Finnan (*http://custom-made.org.uk*) p58, p88
Ed Hicks (*noonard*) p8, p18, p26, p52
Matt Hobbs (*ultrahi*) front cover fence image.
Nick Kaye p15, p16, p46, p47, p48, p72, p73, p77 and back cover image.
Simon Kisner (*www.mistersnappy.co.uk*) p10, p20, p36, p38, p42
Neil Melville-Kenney p2, p5, p30, p32, p34, p43, p50, p64, p74 and
front cover stage image.
Sarah Rider Photography (*www.sarahriderphotography.co.uk*) p25
Charlotte Savill p12, p13, p22, p56, p61, p63, p67, p68, p81
Pete Verity p53, p55, p65
Beezer (*www.beezerphotos.com*) p28, p40, p82
Paul Norris (*www.80srockpics.com*) p6, p78
Mark Simmons (*www.marksimmonsphotography.co.uk*) p44, p70
The Rutland Boughton Music Trust p60

Check out more of their photos on Flickr.

Thanks also to:

Paul Norris who discovered his previously unseen images of
The Smiths at Glastonbury in 1984 in a shoe box in his attic
www.80srockpics.com
The Rutland Boughton Music Trust *www.rutlandboughtonmusictrust.co.uk*

Special thanks to:

Glastonbury Festival staff for tolerating my snooping around, Richard
Jones and all at Tangent Books. Plus Steve, Colin, Lucy and that bloke
who I can't remember the name of who works backstage.

Dedicated to:

You, the mad punter. Rave on.

Please Note:

This is an unofficial book, the publisher and author have agreed to
donate a portion of any profits to the Glastonbury Festival charities.